making simple *felted Jewelry*

Schiffer Publishing Ltd®

4880 Lower Valley Road, Atglen, Pennsylvania 19310

Marsha Fletcher

Dedication

To my best friend and sister, Bonnie,
for her creative inspiration and ongoing support

Other Schiffer Books on Related Subjects:
Felt, Fiber, and Stone: Creative Jewelry Designs & Techniques, 978-0-7643-3668-3, $16.99
Fun Felt Crafts: Penny Rugs & Pretty Things from Recycled Wool, 978-0-7643-3299-9, $12.99
Off-Loom Woven Bead Necklaces, 978-0-7643-3306-4, $19.99

Copyright © 2010 by Marsha Fletcher
Unless otherwise noted, all photos are the property of the author.
Library of Congress Control Number: 2010936268

Designed by Mark David Bowyer
Type set in Fina Heavy / Humanist521 BT

ISBN: 978-0-7643-3570-9
Printed in China

Schiffer Books are available at special discounts for bulk purchases for sales promotions or premiums. Special editions, including personalized covers, corporate imprints, and excerpts can be created in large quantities for special needs. For more information contact the publisher:

Published by Schiffer Publishing Ltd.
4880 Lower Valley Road
Atglen, PA 19310
Phone: (610) 593-1777; Fax: (610) 593-2002
E-mail: Info@schifferbooks.com

For the largest selection of fine reference books on this and related subjects, please visit our web site at:
www.schifferbooks.com
We are always looking for people to write books on new and related subjects. If you have an idea for a book please contact us at the above address.

This book may be purchased from the publisher.
Include $5.00 for shipping.
Please try your bookstore first.
You may write for a free catalog.

In Europe, Schiffer books are distributed by
Bushwood Books
6 Marksbury Ave.
Kew Gardens
Surrey TW9 4JF England
Phone: 44 (0) 20 8392 8585; Fax: 44 (0) 20 8392 9876
E-mail: info@bushwoodbooks.co.uk
Website: www.bushwoodbooks.co.uk

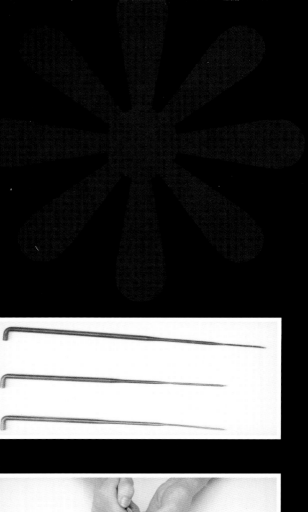

Contents

Acknowledgments

I would like to thank Schiffer Publishing and my editor, Jennifer Marie Savage, for their friendly and helpful guidance. Thank you also to Schiffer's senior editor Douglas Congdon-Martin for his help and expertise in photographing many of the subjects in this book.

I would like to thank my mother, Irene Perkins, and sister, Bonnie Sutton, for their help and support in getting the proper photographs. Bonnie took many of the pictures and, in April 2009, the three of us took a five-day working vacation to visit Schiffer Publishing close to beautiful Lancaster County, Pennsylvania. We all had a wonderful time — the staff at Schiffer was very friendly, making it great experience for all of us.

I would also like to thank the models pictured in this book for taking time out of their busy schedules: Courtney Rowland, Tricia Osborn, Holly Dastalfo, and sisters Helen and Sophie Sibol.

Foreword

I grew up on a farm in Central Lower Michigan in the 1960s. I had what I would consider to be a fairly comfortable young life: a family that loved me, plenty of good food, clothes that fit me, and a clean warm bed. The problem was that I lived on what I call a "sterile farm." We grew potatoes… I wanted horses.

I have been totally obsessed with animals for as long as I can remember. All my imaginary friends had four legs. I "daydreamed" and "doodled" my way through grade school, using my bigger than life imagination, and I exposed my "make believe friends" to the real world using my second love — art.

I have always enjoyed trying new and different types of art forms. Since needle felting was introduced to me, no other medium can compare to the colors and textures that are available for this craft. (In all fairness to my parents, they finally did give in and buy me a pony. Thank-you Mom and Dad!)

My sister, Bonnie, who has been a long time breeder of rare and endangered sheep, introduced me to needle felting. She showed me how easy it was to bind the wool fibers with the felting needle by simply piercing the wool hundreds of times until the wool took a desired shape. At first I thought the process was very simple and even seemed a bit on the boring side.

"That is amazing!" I lied, not wanting to hurt her feelings. When it was time to leave, Bonnie gave me a small bag of different wool samples and a couple felting needles. I took the wool and needles home and put them away, thinking to myself, "I'll try needle felting someday if I have time... maybe."

One day, about a year later, I came across the bag of wool and felting needles in the closet and decided to give another go at it. First, I tried to form a simple object. I was quickly fascinated with the huge amount of control that you can have with this very simple process.

Since that day I haven't stopped needle felting — I am hooked. It is truly amazing! I have done some needle felting almost every day and taught myself my own techniques by experimenting with different fibers, wools, textures, and colors.

Jim and me (1966)

My husband and I live on a small farm that includes many types of animals; two dogs, six cats, three miniature horses, two miniature donkeys, a few chickens, a llama, and we have recently added a small flock of Shetland sheep to help support my wool fetish. I have learned by using the wool from my sheep and llama that I can create and sell fiber art. I can support my hobby from doing what I love most.

Lola and Tutu from our flock.

This book is designed to teach some basic needle felting techniques. It may not instantly transform you into a master fiber artist, but the skills you learn will be an excellent foundation for your new needle felting craft. Hopefully this book will inspire you for many wonderful years of felting and working with natural fibers.

The Fiber Artist's Wool Shopping Experience

The bells clatter. You hear the screen door slam at your heels and realize it's too late — you are now inside.

"Hello!" you call out. There is something about surrounding yourself among a fresh smelling roving in a rainbow of colors and textures. Wonderfully crimped fiber has long been known to have strange effects on the nesting portion of the female brain. In some cases, vertigo, confusion, and memory lapses have been reported. You feel light-headed as you wander among the gorgeous fibers. You hear something. "Are those bagpipes?" you ask yourself out loud.

A voice without a form calls out to you from a large bin of wool. "Excuse me madam..." The lovely locks coax you to turn back, just to take closer look. You are now totally convinced that you have lost your mind! You are not here today to buy a soft ivory fleece, you remind yourself repeatedly, as you force yourself to continue on. Yet there are so many oversized bolts of brilliantly colored premium wool top: blues, golds, reds, and greens. Amazing!

Just like a paint store, no shade or tone is forgotten. Every bolt of fiber is neatly arranged in a creative and organized manner. Suddenly you feel as if you may faint. You cling to your purse, clutching it to your wildly beating heart. A soft fresh breeze of spring air floats though the screen door and cools the perspiration on your sweltering forehead. You feel slightly better. Then it catches your eye. You cry out, "Wow! Is that mohair?" It stirs the senses with creativity! The wonderful feel of the texture! The color is amazing! The possibilities are endless! It's all too much, and that's it, it's all she wrote... It's all you remember. You never knew what hit you. The next thing you know you are driving down the road, heading home, penniless, with fifty-six pounds of various colors and textures of wool fibers!

DISCLAIMER: While I cannot verify the actuality of the above report, I can tell you that with needle felting, unlike many crafts, only a few inexpensive tools and materials are actually needed to experience this wool art. Just as a safety precaution, though, may I suggest to the wool fiber shopper, to leave the store at once if even the slightest tune of bagpipes are heard. Run away... Run!

Introduction

Wool Felting: The process that takes place when the microscopic scales on the wool fiber interlock and tightly mat with each other, bonding the fiber.

History or Mystery of Felt?

Everywhere we look today in the world of arts and crafts, it seems that wool felt is the new trendy fad! Actually, we should think of it as: "What is old is new again."

Over the years rare felt artifacts have surfaced from around the world, like pieces to a puzzle, and archaeologist are continuously trying to fill in the pieces that have vanished with time and decay.

Felting methods were used long before early man had invented any other techniques of spinning fiber or weaving with looms. Wool felt was used in many Shamanic and religious rituals such as the Tibetan wedding carpet, as well as for dolls that were believed to protect the well-being of the family. Felt was sometimes used to make shrouds for corpses and for tapestries that hung on the walls in the tombs of the wealthy.

Fragments of a very old wool felt painting were found on the wall of a tomb in Turkey dating back to 6500 BC. The oldest known wool textile that was discovered in Europe was dated around 1500 BC. It was a wool boot found preserved in a Danish bog. Evidence of another example of early felt was found preserved by permafrost in a tomb in Siberia; it was dated about 600 AD. Recently, a felt hat and boot liners were discovered in a tomb near the western desert in China — these artifacts date back to 1400 to 1200 BC.

For several centuries, the Mongolian nomadic people have lived in yurts, which are portable tent-like houses. These yurts were first shaped like tepees with pole supports up though the center. Today thousands of Mongolians, Russians, and Siberians still live in felt wool yurts, but now they are much larger and more elaborate. The portable wool houses are large and round with a collapsible frame along the outer edge. Some yurts are four felt-layers thick for weather insulation. The temperature inside them can remain tolerable even through the most extreme climate conditions — from -40 below zero to a sweltering 100 degrees!

Wool felt was not discovered just one time, but accidentally rediscovered many times over the centuries around the world. One example is the story of Saint Clement and Saint Christopher, which relates that while fleeing from persecution, the men packed their sandals with wool to prevent blisters and by the end of their journey their movement and sweat had felted the wool into socks!

Since wool tends to decay over thousands of years, ideal conditions must be present to preserve the wool fibers. Because of this, we may never truly know when early men first wore wool felt socks on their feet.

Techniques of Hand Felting

I prefer the dry method of hand needle felting because it is easy to stop and start with less mess during normal daily interruptions. Needle felting, although relaxing, can be time consuming.

It would be interesting to combine two or more of the methods described below into one project. You could begin by wet felting and then, after it is completely dry, switch to needle felting to finish the details by either machine or hand needle felting. Never limit your personal creativity. Inspiration is everywhere...especially in the color and textures of your everyday life.

Wet Felting

The oldest form of felt, it's a process of matting together wool fibers by using hot water, heat, and friction. The finished fabric can vary in thickness, texture, and suppleness. The wool wrapped feet under the sandals would be an example of wet felting.

Knitted Wet Felted

This newer technique is popular for felting knitted purses and hats. The item is knitted with wool yarn and then washed in the washing machine, resulting in the wool shrinking and bonding the yarns into attractive felt. This method was obviously discovered though someone's misfortune of a wool sweater that was improperly cared for.

Needle Felting by Hand

It is safe to say that it is less than 130 years old when the felting needle was invented. It has increased in popularity in the last twenty years. It is a done by using clean and processed wool fiber and a special barbed needle. The wool fibers are connected together by simply piercing the wool repeatedly hundreds of times until the wool sculpture takes the desired shape.

Needle Felting by Machine

This method can be done using a sewing machine with a special felting attachment. Special felting machines are also available in most stores that sell sewing machines.

These pumpkins were needle felted by Brandon Sutton.

This purse was made using the wet felting method.

Section One:
Tools and Materials

I suggest that you, the artist, should keep everything that is needed for the project you are working on together in a box or container. One with a lid is best. It also would be ideal to start a fiber journal, to note your favorite fibers and needle shapes and gauges. The box should be safely stored away from pets and young children until you are able to resume work on your wool art piece.

Where to purchase supplies? I would like to invite everyone to visit our website for a virtual tour of our 1920s farm, see what is happening in the studio, and shop at the farm store. Everything needed for the projects in this book and more can be easily purchased by "Shopping Cart" from our website. Or simply drop us an email with questions or comments. We can be found at: Wool-In Legends Farm & Studio, 7100 Vickerville Road, Edmore, Michigan 48829. To reach us by phone, call 989-427-3740, or email us at wool-in-legends.com or sheepythyme.com.

I hope that you too will admire wool fiber and enjoy working with wool as much as I do!

Chapter One

The Felting Needle

During the Industrial Revolution of the late 1800s, the felting needle was invented for factory machines. The felting machines were used to make batting and insulations from recycled materials, such as old shredded wool clothing, animal hair, and odds and ends of scrap wool.

Today the felting needle is still used much the same way in industrial fiber mills. Felt is made from an assortment or blend of animal or plant origin and synthetic fibers and scraps to keep the cost down. Large automated tables holding huge steel plates with thousands of barbed felting needles pierce the various fiber scraps repeatedly. Some tables also have a second felting plate dense with the felting needle poking upward through the bottom side of the felt until the desired thickness and texture is achieved. The felt is often cut into endless shapes with dye press or sometimes sold on huge industrial bolts.

This factory process sounds rather unappealing! No wonder those so-called "felt squares" in the craft stores are so paper-like, stiff, and lifeless — they are made from recycled junk of who knows what! However, it is good to know that there are uses for synthetic fiber scraps other than adding even more to the local landfills.

Hand needle felting in the home started with mending socks or sweaters. Needle felting, as we know it today, began to catch on as a craft in the 1980s when the first needle felting books were published.

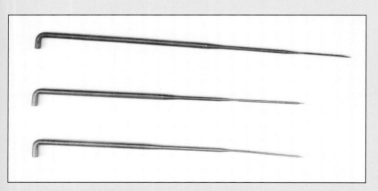

These are the most common sizes of the felting needles.

The Felt Needle Today

Today, felting needles come in many sizes and shapes. All the needles have several tiny barbed hooks that point downward. The barbed hooks grasp the single strands of fiber and pushes them together, locking the scales of the fibers together. The fibers are released from the barbs when the felting needle is pulled back. This simple hand movement is repeated again and again.

This process may sound boring or too repetitive to the beginner, but it is far from being so. Although felting is a very forgiving art, each stroke affects the project's end results, just as a painter's strokes on her canvas.

Felting needles are normally about three inches long depending on the manufacturer. The needle shaft is available in many shapes and sizes; the triangle star and conical are the most common. The number of barbs and their location on the needle may vary. Star shaped needles have more barbs because they have an extra surface.

The size of the needle diameter is referred to as the gage — common sizes include 36 to 40. The lower the number the more coarse the needle shaft.

- Gage #36 — This needle is used for rough felting or working with a coarser fiber; it will leave unwanted holes in the felt.
- Gage #38 — This is the basic needle most often used. It leaves smaller holes than the #36.

- Gage #40 — This needle is used for finishing off a project and the fine details. They leave the least visible holes in the finished product.

Please keep in mind when you are purchasing felting needles you might want buy several at a time. The finer the needle, the more easily they are broken. I would like to recommend to the beginner that they try the different needle sizes and experiment with various kinds of fibers for different results. If you decide to buy just one basic size needle, the #38 triangle is a good choice.

These are examples of tools that hold multiple needles.
Left: holding four felting needles; right: holding nine felting needles.

Chapter Two:
Fascinating Wool Fiber

Wool is a very useful and interesting fiber. As a natural and renewable resource, its remarkable qualities cannot be duplicated. Wool is strong, warm, resilient, and weatherproof.

Wool serves as a protective insulated coat for sheep. The fibers are hygroscopic, which means it has the ability to readily absorb and give off moisture through the microscopic scales on the outside of the wool fiber shaft. The scales are able to open and close to warm and cool the sheep's body temperature. It keeps the sheep warm in the winter and cool in the summer, and the sheep's lanolin coating keeps its body dry. When the fleece is wet, the sheep's body temperature is always five degrees warmer. Wool has a very high porosity and is able to hold one-third of its weight in water. It is because of all of this that hikers and skiers know that wearing wool is their best protection against hypothermia.

Another amazing quality is that wool has a natural flame retardant. It ignites at higher temperatures than cotton and most synthetics. It does not drip or melt. Flash flaming never occurs with wool, which forms a char that insulates it and self-extinguishes. It also gives off less toxic gases and smoke than other fibers, which often makes wool the choice of fabric for carpeting and seats on airplanes and other forms of public transportation.

Wool is also usually the specified fiber worn by firefighters and other occupations where fire is a danger. Some synthetics are fireproof, however unlike wool, they do not insulate the body and the flesh may burn through the clothing. Wool is also static resistant since it holds moisture inside the fiber shaft and the fabric does not spark or hold static electricity. Contrary to popular belief, wool is considered by the medical profession to be hypoallergenic.

Sheep Breeds and their Fleece

Sheep are thought to have been domesticated for over 10,000 years! There are more breeds of sheep than any other livestock species. There are over two hundred distinct breeds, though others claim that, with newly developed breeds, there are about 1,000 sheep breeds worldwide. Sheep are primarily bred for their wool, though some are bred for food such as meat or dairy. Many breeds serve multi purposes.

So many different sheep breeds mean a huge amount of fiber to choose from. It would be very difficult to test all the wool breeds for their felting qualities, even if they were readily available in the United States. Although many types of wool will felt, some breeds of sheep wool will work much better than others for the particular project that you are working on. When I first started felting, I thought that I only wanted to use a medium fiber thickness for everything. Shetland and Icelandic are my favorite fibers to felt with. While I still feel these wools needle felt very nicely, it would be a huge mistake to not experiment with different fiber blends, textures, and colors once you have learned the felting basics.

The wool quality is determined by the following factors: fiber diameter, strength, crimp, color, yield, and staple length. The fiber diameter is the single most important characteristic in judging quality and price.

The Modern Wool Breeds

Sheep that have been bred for their wool production tend to be smaller with a white face and white wool. White wool can be dyed and is more consistent than natural colored wool, and these wool breeds are at least distantly related to the champion European breed, the Merino. However, they seem to have lost the coarse outer coat of their wild ancestors in exchange for more of a soft insulated inner coat that is good for spinning and other wool working.

Best Wool Producing Hybrids

American Cormo	Rambouillet
East Friesian	Corriedale
Booroola Merino	Targhee
Panama	Debouuillet
Columbia	Deliane Merino

Second-Tier Wool Breeds

Bluefaced Leicester	Southdown
Montadale	Clun Forest
Romney	Polypay
Border Leicester	Texel
North Country Cheviot	Dorset
Shropshire	Romedale
Cheviot	Lincoln
Perendale	

Charming Breeds

These are most often referred to as unimproved, rare, antique, or heirloom breeds. This special group of purebreds should not be lost and forgotten. The numbers of these flocks have drastically dropped as new and more profitable hybrid sheep have been developed.

There is a soft spot in my heart for this special group of sheep. Some plants and animals should be left as they are, like the flavor of heirloom tomatoes and the wonderful smell of grandma's antique rose brush. These breeds of sheep probably will not make you rich by producing large expensive fleeces and you may not be feasting on huge legs of lamb, but these sheep are hearty and they are lower maintenance than many of the newer breeds. They also have maintained some their wild survival instincts. Since they are so called "unimproved," they can survive extreme weather conditions. In general, they have fewer problems with lambing than many hybrids.

Cotswool	Romanov
Karakul	Mountain Welsh
St. Croix	Icelandic
Finnsheep	Scottish Blackface
Navajo-Churro	Wiltshire Horn
Tunis	Jacob
Gulf Coast Native	Shetland

Even though old breeds are small and have smaller fleeces or less meat than modern hybrids, these breeds that time have left behind are often preferred by spinners, knitters, and fiber artists. It seems there is some comfort in clinging to a few old ways. Also they provide a wide range of natural color not found in the new and improved breeds. These old-fashioned breeds add an Old Country charm to homespun arts and crafts.

Choosing the Right Wool Fiber

Choosing quality fiber for your project is important. The wool fiber of each sheep breed has its own distinct characteristics. Some sheep, such as the Merino, have very fine and soft wool with about one hundred crimps per inch and many scales. Both crimps and scales are needed for the best spinning and felting results. After the wool is cleaned, washed, and carded, the wool appears straighter. It has a slight luster, as well as a cotton-like appearance.

Steer clear of coarse glossy wools for needle felting, such as the Boarder Leicester. Straighter hair-like wools have fewer crimps. Some coarse wool only have one or two crimps per inch and fewer scales, which makes them difficult to felt. The large fiber shafts can be felted, but takes much more effort. For that reason I do not recommend their use to the beginner needle felter.

Long wools take dyes beautifully. The coarse wool stays glossy and the fibers look almost glass coated, which means they have fewer scales. They make a pretty but coarse yarn, which wears long and makes beautiful long-lasting rugs! Though they may not felt easily, these make pretty doll hair!

Super fine wool fiber — like that of the Merino — is known to work well for wet felting, but not so well for needle felting. The delicate fibers can at times be too soft and will break too easily.

However, others can be too wire-like and coarse and refuse to felt. Objects using a very fine needle, such as a #40 gage, will take on a beautiful soft look of velvet or chenille.

Large objects should normally be done with a coarser wool fiber. Coarse fibers tend to hide needle marks and is more forgiving. In addition to sheep wool felting, other felt-able fibers are the llama, alpaca, camel, yak, buffalo, angora rabbit, goat, cotton, silk, bamboo, soy, and even pretty dog hair!

I have thought about exploring other natural fibers, such as the delicate seed from milkweed and Cottonwood trees, and blending their soft silk-like fibers into wool fibers. I have rescued horsetail hairs from grooming brushes for "whiskers" on my wool sculptures. I also have used wool yarn, recycled and re-purposed soft chunks of wool felt, and even strips of rug hooking wool. Using several different textures of various fibers can have a beautiful end result.

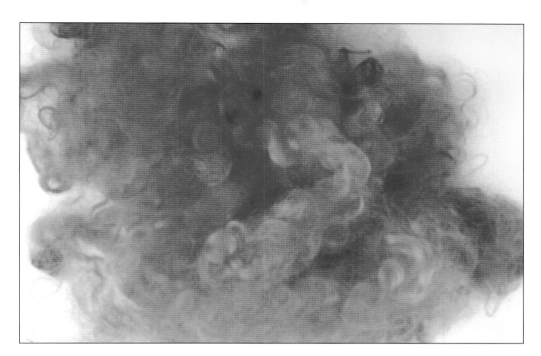

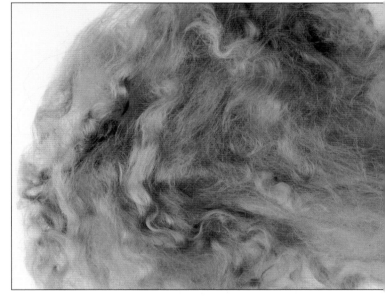

I feel that when you are hand felting, unlike factory felt, it is like baking a cake. When you are baking a cake, if you use top quality ingredients like farm fresh eggs, premium flour, and real vanilla, you will probably get a much better cake. In contrast, if you use expired grocery store eggs, two-year-old flour, and imitation vanilla, it takes the same amount of work, but the end result is inferior.

Felting cakes... They look almost good enough to eat!

When you are planning a fiber project, choose an interesting fiber that pleases your eye. It should be fluffy, clean, and a color that you like; if it's tacky, that indicates the wool was not washed properly. The wool should be free of mats and vegetable matter. Also, be conscious of guard hairs and the coarse, wire-like fibers.

Protecting Yourself

A piece of high-density foam at least two inches thick is needed to place beneath the wool project as you, the felter, work. The foam is used to rest the wool subject on as the felting needle shapes and sculpts it. The foam also protects the work surface, increases the shelf life of the felting needles, and also helps prevent unwanted body piercings!

Foam work surface for needle felting.

Chapter Three:

Pincushion

Practice Makes Perfect

This pincushion is made from the fiber of my gray llama and white Shetland, which was a light gray wool blend. The fiber was divided into three portions and hand dyed-over in three separate dyes: teal, gold, and red.

This fun and easy project is designed to teach you about the different gages of the felting needles. You will test several needle sizes — 36 to 40 gage, both the star and triangle.

Pincushion for felting needles.

What to Do

1. Begin by firmly winding the roving into a ball of wool. Make sure to use the foam pad under the wool felt of each layer as you wind the ball.

2. With the wool ball placed on the foam pad, practice gently piercing it with different sizes of needles. Be sure to keep the needle straight — do not bend it, as the tips are fragile and will break off easily. Also, do not stab the wool with too much force. You will break your needle, you will not be in control of the desired wool shape, and you may stab your finger!

3. Firmly squeeze the wool with your fingers and secure the wool with several firm pokes of the felting needle in that same area to keep it in place. Remember, the barbs are only on the tips of the felting needles. Also, always use firm, controlled strokes while holding the needle straight.

4. Continue to wrap the roving around the ball. Then place the fiber ball on the foam pad; hold the ball securely with your fingers on the outer edges and poke in a firm, repeated motion while slightly moving the needle along the surface of the ball (and staying clear of your fingers!).

5. Now, squeeze the ball into the desired shape — continue to squeeze and poke. Repeat this process until the ball is the desired size.

Try all the needle sizes — notice how each needle catches the fibers differently? This exercise will help you feel how tight the wool will become with your first needle-felted object. The more you pierce the cushion, notice how much smaller and firmer it becomes.

Decorate as desired. I made a braid from wool roving for the top of my pincushion. I tightly coiled it and secured it to the pincushion with a felting needle. I also added a small ring shaped hanger for small scissors.

TIP: Felting needles rust quite quickly when you are not using them, so here's what to do: Mix 1/8 of a cup almond oil with a few drops of lavender or rosemary essential oils in a small glass spray bottle. Shake the bottle to blend the oils. Mist the needle cushions; repeat the misting occasionally as needed. (You can use plain baby oil if you prefer.) Using this special wool cushion keeps the needle sharp and ready to use. Also, it smells wonderful!

Let's Make Jewelry

When you learn to design your own one-of-a-kind piece of jewelry, simple outfits will become outstanding! Each piece can be custom created to suit the personality of the individual wearing it. Use fiber in colors to match existing wardrobes. It is also the perfect time to express yourself with a new look. With felt, you can go as crazy with the design as you dare! Since only small amounts of wool roving are needed when making jewelry, it is a good time to use up wool scraps and yarns.

Chapter Four

Felt Bead Necklace

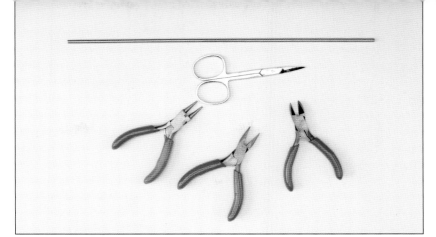

Gather the following tools and materials: small scissors, jewelry tools, pliers, wire cutters, and crimper.

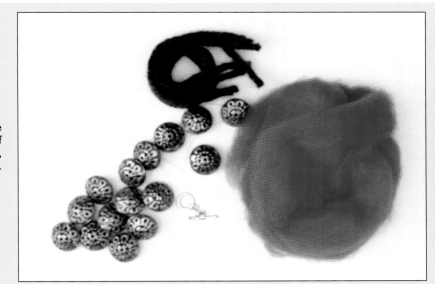

Materials you will need are a half-ounce of wool roving, several large beads of your choice, 25 inches of jewelry wire, two crimping beads, and a toggle closure.

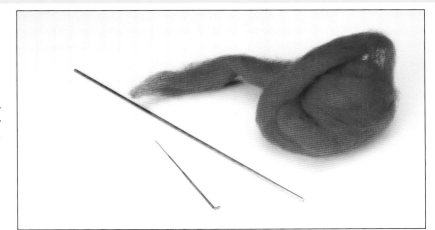

You will also need a felting needle, a heavy gauge wire, or a thin metal rod. The diameter of the wire will be the size of the bead hole.

To begin your first bead, pull off a small piece of the wool (approximately two inches long).

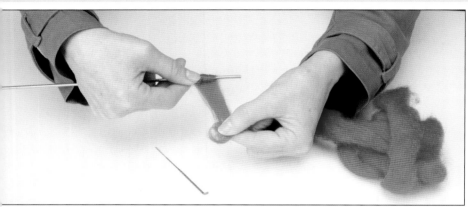

Wrap the wool around the rod, pulling the wool roving firm and smooth.

To begin the felting process, use the felting needle to poke the wool. Pierce the bead several times to hold it together.

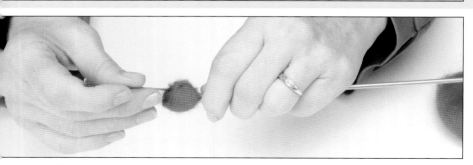

Add another layer of wool over the first wrap tightly and felt it with the needle to the first layer. Repeat the process until the bead is at the desired size. Firmly felt by continuing to poke the bead until it is round and smooth.

To decorate, cut a one- to two-inch piece of yarn and separate the strands.

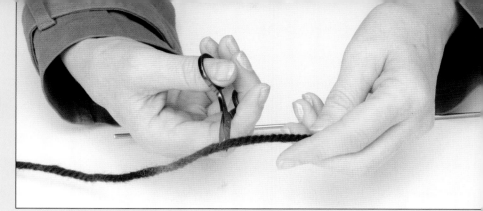

Apply the stands to the bead surface with the felting needle.

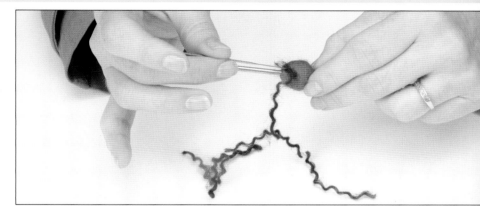

This bead is complete with embellishments.

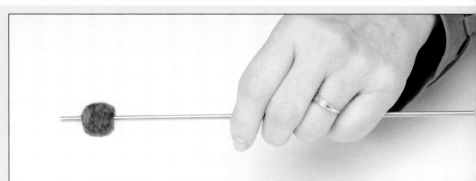

Repeat the process until you have enough beads for the desired length for your necklace.

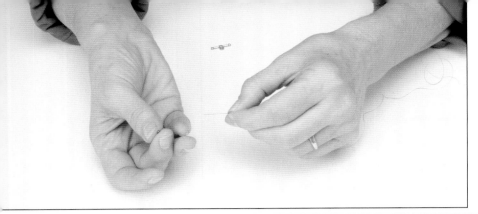

Cut the desired length of beading wire (I used 22 inches) and begin stringing the beads by placing a crimping bead on one end.

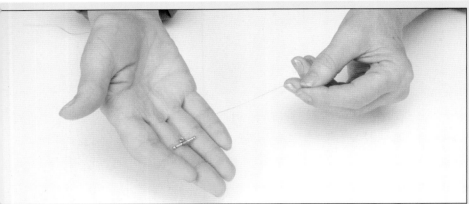

Add the male end of the toggle clasp next to the crimper bead...

...and place the end of the wire through the crimp bead.

Pinch it closed with the crimper tool or a small pair of pliers.

String the desired bead pattern. (Here large silver beads were used as spacers.)

Finish the string by attaching the female end of the toggle with a crimper bead and then trim off the extra wire.

You are finished!

Chapter Five:

Wool Coil Rope Necklace

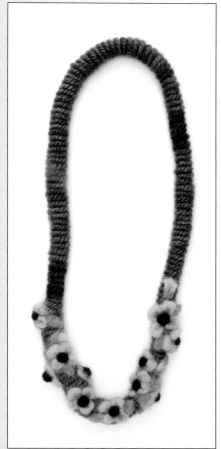

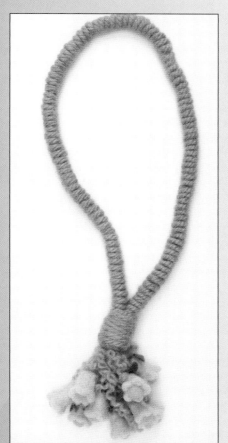

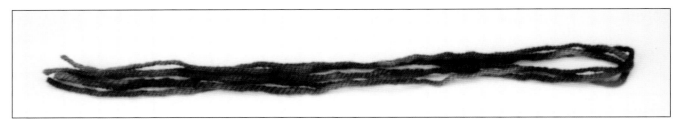

Begin with three strands of yard long 3-ply rug yarn (only 100 percent wool will work for this project).

Tie a sample knot in one end of the three stands of yarn to hold them firmly in place while you work.

Take another section of yarn, about 18 inches long, and begin to wrap the yarn next to the knot securely with the felting needle. Wrap as uniformly as possible and felt with the needle to hold it in place.

Continue the coiling
and felting.

Repeat this process. Try to keep
the loops evenly sized, felting them
in place as you go. Roll the coil,
felting it firmly on all sides.

When the first section of yarn is
completed, add a new section.
Join the second section of yarn
to where the first one left off.
Felt it firmly into place. No
tying or sewing is necessary —
the felting process will hold it
securely in place. Repeat the
process until the coil reaches
about two inches from the end.

When you're finished, trim the core yarn pieces so you can join them.

To join the two ends of the necklace, use the long yarn strand. Continue coiling and felting, connecting them together.

Felt the coil firmly into a seamless piece.

Now the coil is ready for embellishments.

Embellishing the Coil Necklace

This is where you can really experiment and express your style!

The Bell Flower

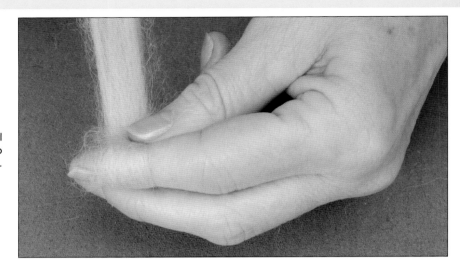

Begin by wrapping a small piece of wool around the tip of your finger three times.

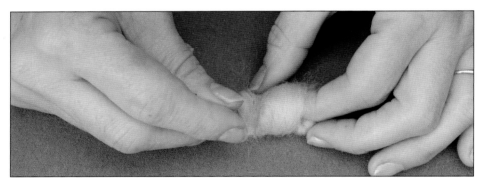

Now shape the bell by placing your finger in the open end of the bell and close the base at the tip of your finger.

Use caution not to poke your finger. With the needle laying on the foam, close the small end at your fingertip.

The bell is now taking shape; lay it aside while you shape a yellow center for the flower. Using a small piece of yellow roving, wrap it twice around your finger. Then slide it off your finger and shape it into a ball with the felting needle.

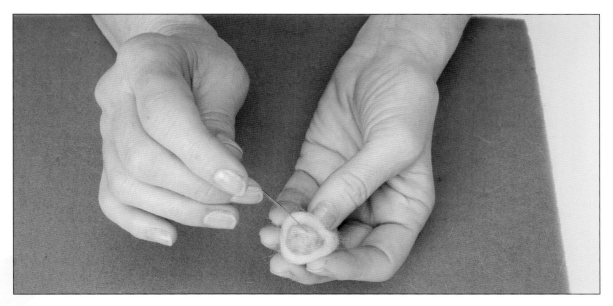

Place the yellow ball into the center of the bell and felt it. Use care to leave extra blue roving outside the center to form petals on the tips.

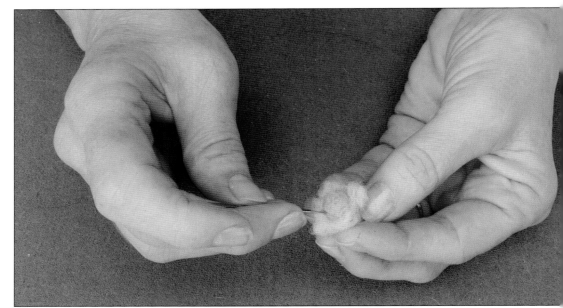

Add several bells by felting into place any way you like.

Here yarn scraps were used as vines — they were attached by needle felting. Decorative yarn was wrapped and felted to add interest to the piece.

The finished necklace.

Adding a Needle Felt Pattern

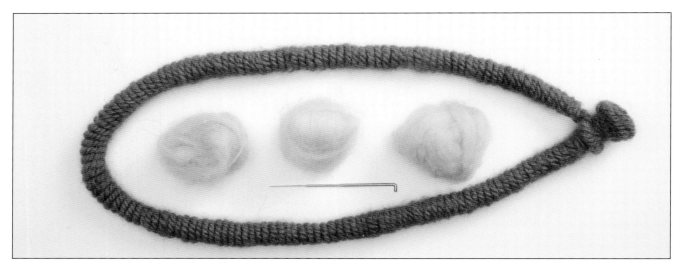

Add felting decorations on the chain using your felting needle.

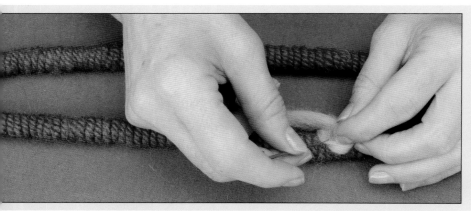

To make a simple flower, wrap a small piece around the tip of your finger. Slide the wool off the end of your finger and felt it onto the necklace. Shape a small petal by felting it onto the chain. Repeat three times, making four petals.

Using the same technique, form the centers of the flower.

Shape the center and felt it into place.

You will form and attach leaves for the flowers in the same way — use your fingers and the felt needle to shape them.

To give the piece an extra dimension, more colors can be added for shading. Lavender wool is being added for contrast in this picture.

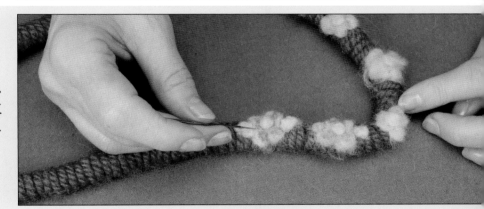

Here an outline of the technique being used.

Add as much or as little embellishment as you like.

Chapter Six:

Double Wrap Wool Bracelet

The materials needed for this project are wool roving, wool rug hooking strips, and wool rug yarn. Variegated yarn was used for this bracelet, however you may use any wool yarn and a six-inch piece of thin wire to form a circle. Twist the wire ends together. Note: the wire ring should be two inches larger than your wrist so that the finished bracelet will slide over your hand.

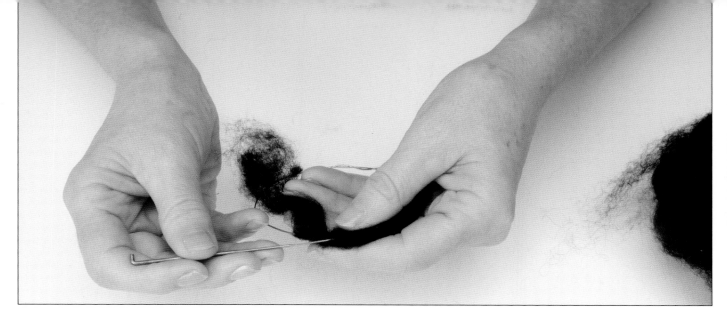

Begin by wrapping the wool roving around the wire circle and felting needle. Felt it with the needle holding it into place.

Felt around the entire wire frame. When the first layer is completely covered, repeat with a second layer — the bracelet should be felted firmly. It will become hard. At this point, the bracelet is still not full enough. Another layer of wool is added for more volume.

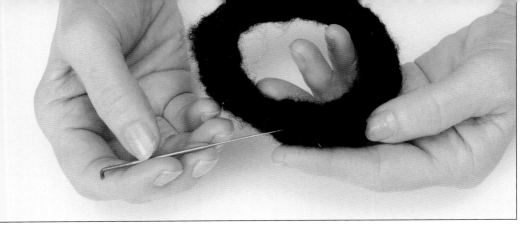

Use the same method of wrapping and felting you have been using in the other projects until you have the thickness you like.

Now the bracelet is ready to decorate.

Begin applying rug hooking strips by felting the end of the first strip into place. Wrap firmly into place. Overlapping and covering the bracelet for a new textured look, felt into place.

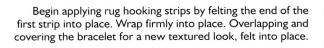

Continue to wrap strips butting ends. When adding a new strip, felt them securely down.

Cut wool yarn and decorate by placing and felting the yarn securely where you like.

The finished bracelet.

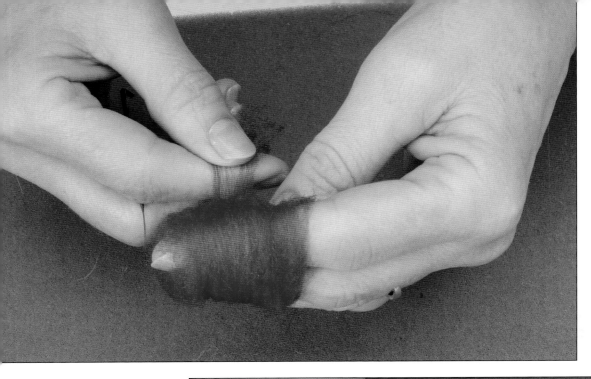

Begin by wrapping wool around two fingers.

Use the felting needle to felt and shape the petal firmly into the desired petal shape.

  52

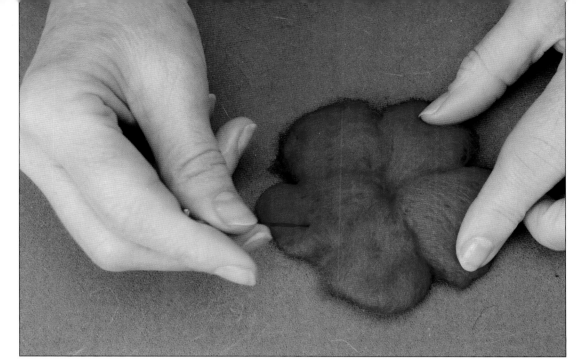

Repeat four more times — make a total of five petals for the bottom layer.

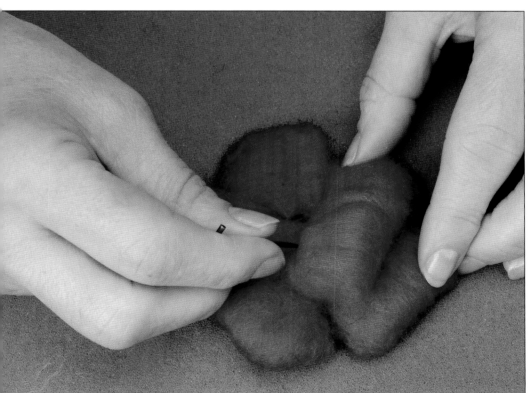

Arrange the petals into a flower and needle felt them together at the center.

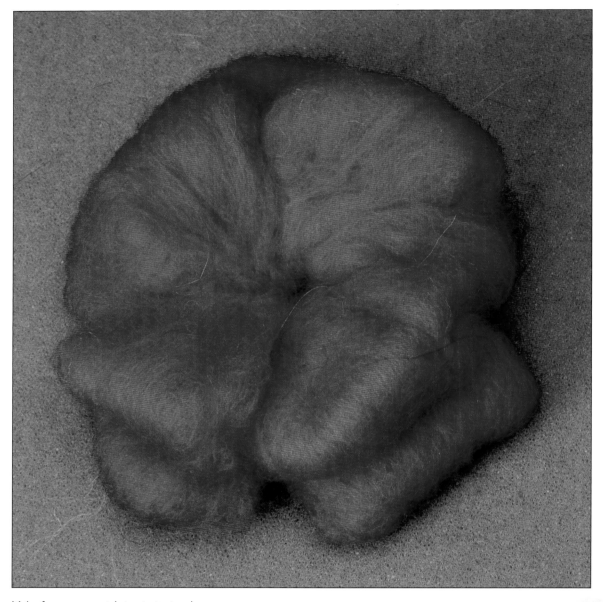

Make four more petals to start a top layer.

Arrange and attach the new petals to the center of the bottom layer of the flower. Hold up the petals. Keep them separated when felting the layers together.

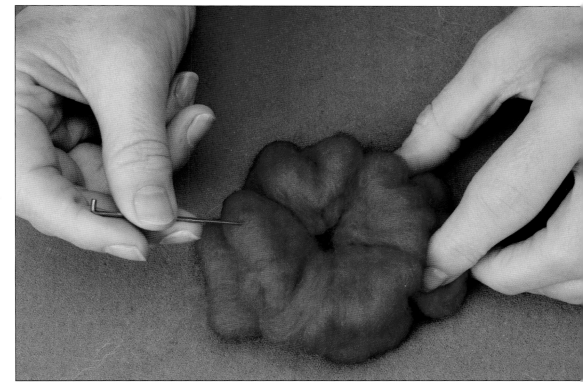

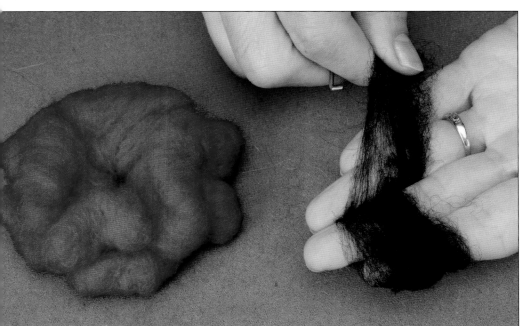

To make a flower center, wrap the wool roving around your finger three times. Slide it onto the foam pad and felt it into a button shape.

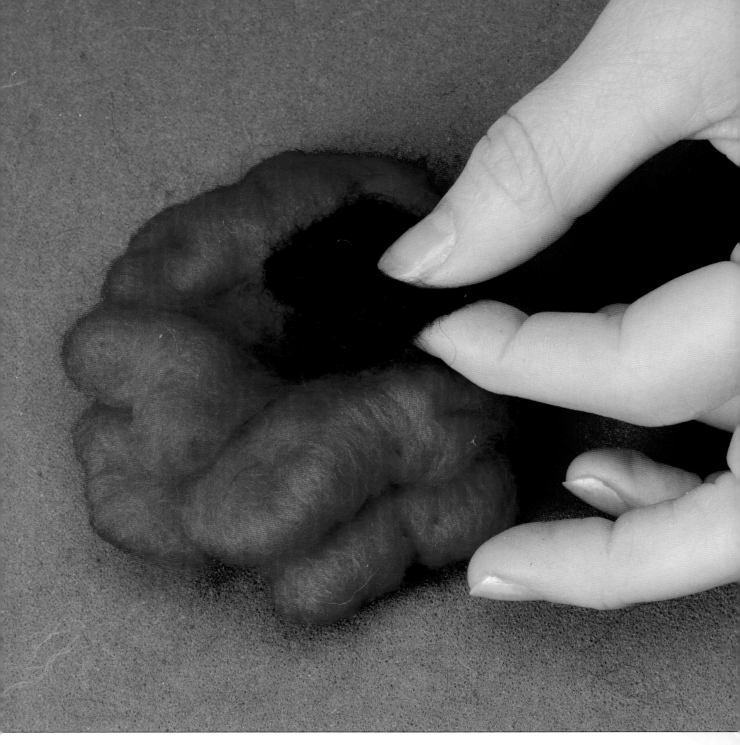

Arrange the center of the flower and attach it in place using the felting method.

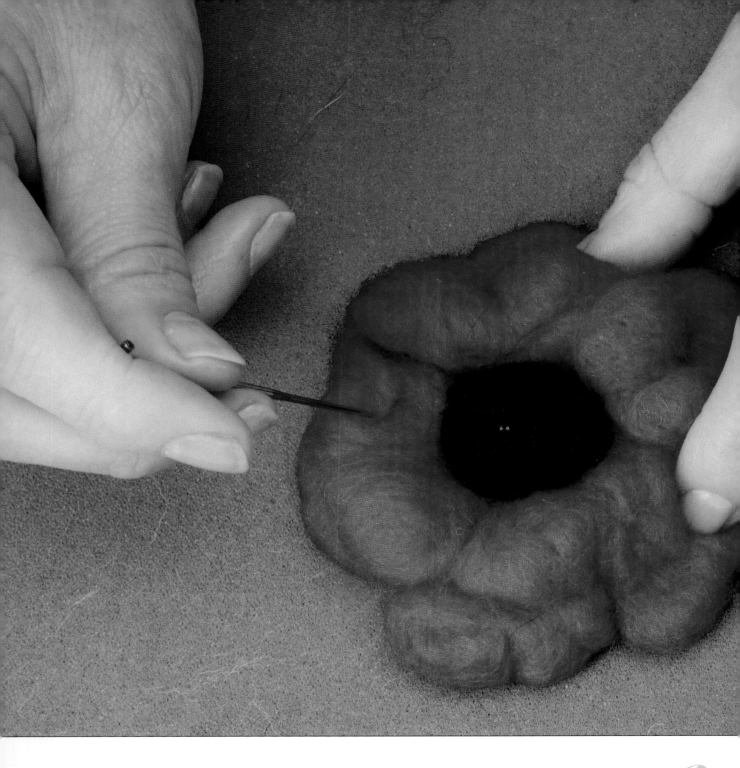

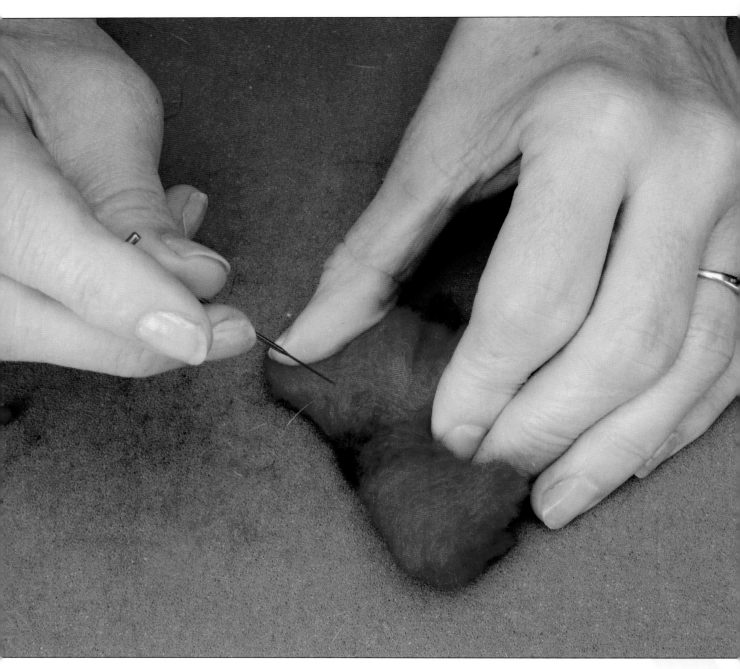

Fold the flower and needle felt completely through the center. Make sure that all the layers are well connected.

Leaves can be
added if you like.

Gallery